HIROSHIMA

HIROSHIMA

A

NOVELLA BY
LAURENCE YEP

SCHOLASTIC INC.
New York Toronto London Auckland Sydney

Copyright © 1995 by Laurence Yep.
All rights reserved. Published by Scholastic Inc.
Printed in the United States of America. 113

ISBN 0-439-06417-1

SCHOLASTIC, READ 180, and associated logos and designs are trademarks and/or registered trademarks of Scholastic Inc.
LEXILE is a trademark of MetaMetrics, Inc.

X 94256

20 21   113   17   16

In memory of Yoshiko Uchida

CONTENTS

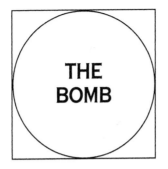

THE
BOMB

Early in the morning of August 6, 1945, a big American bomber roars down the runway on a tiny island called Tinian. The pilot is Colonel Tibbets. He has named the plane after his mother, Enola Gay. On a routine mission, a B-29 would carry 4000 to 16,000 pounds of bombs. The *Enola Gay* is on a special mission. It carries a single

1

bomb. It is an atom bomb that weighs 8900 pounds. Everyone hopes the atom bomb will finally end a long and horrible war.

☙

Four years before, on December 7, 1941, Japanese planes attacked American ships in Hawaii without warning. Caught by surprise, many ships and planes were wrecked at the naval base, Pearl Harbor. The United States declared war on Japan and Japan's ally, Germany. With other countries, they fight a war called World War II.

By 1945, Germany has given up. Only Japan fights on. But the United States has a secret weapon — the atom bomb. Nothing is as powerful and as awful. The atom bomb is so terrible that

THE BOMB

the United States hopes it will make Japan stop fighting.

☙

Two other bombers follow the *Enola Gay*. These planes only carry cameras and special instruments to measure the explosion. Together the three bombers turn over the Pacific Ocean and speed through the darkness toward Japan.

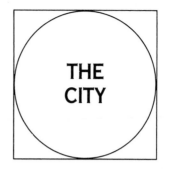

THE CITY

It is only seven o'clock in the morning, but the air is already hot and muggy in Hiroshima. People go to work. Children hurry to school. Some soldiers and women go out with baskets to shop. A peddler wheels his cart carefully through the crowd. A colonel exercises his white horse. There are about 320,000 people in Hiroshima that morning.

Two sisters walk sleepily in the crowd. Riko is sixteen and her little sister, Sachi, is twelve. They have stayed up all night hiding from American bombers. Up until now, though, the airplanes have always bombed other cities. Some people believe that Hiroshima is so beautiful that the Americans have decided to spare it.

Riko and Sachi stop by a shrine. They say a prayer for their father, who is in the army. Looking at the calm, forgiving face of Buddha, they begin to feel at peace.

🪷

An American bomber flies ahead of the *Enola Gay* and its companions. This bomber is called the *Straight Flush*. It will check the weather over Hiroshima. If there are clouds over Hiroshima, the *Straight Flush* will tell the *Enola Gay* to attack another city.

The crew of the *Straight Flush* scans the sky anxiously for Japanese fighter planes. However, the Japanese are saving their airplanes for the invasion that everyone expects. So there are no Japanese planes today.

At first, the *Straight Flush* only sees clouds. Then, the crew spots a big hole in the clouds directly over Hiroshima. The sunlight pours right through the hole on to the city.

Green hills surround the city and the seven rivers shine like ribbons.

Hiroshima is a perfect target.

THE CITY

The *Straight Flush* tells the *Enola Gay* to continue to Hiroshima.

✿

In the meantime, down below in Hiroshima, someone spots the *Straight Flush* and sounds the alarm.

The siren shrieks in short blasts. Everywhere, people stop whatever they are doing. A streetcar rumbles to a halt. Its passengers run for the air-raid shelter.

Sachi and Riko leave the shrine and join the others. "Put on your hood, Sachi," Riko tells her. From their emergency bags, the two sisters pull out air-raid hoods. Putting them over their heads, they tie them tight. If the bombs start fires, the hoods are supposed to protect them from burning sparks.

With the other people, they go down the steps to hide in the darkness.

However, the *Straight Flush* passes harmlessly over the city.

WORK

When the *Straight Flush* finally leaves, the siren announces that it is safe. Breathing sighs of relief, the people leave the bomb shelters. They hurry to finish their interrupted chores. They go back to their homes to cook breakfast. The shopkeepers reopen their stores. The streetcars rumble along the tracks again.

Everyone believes that they are safe now. They do not think more bombers will come so soon after the *Straight Flush*.

Sachi takes off her hood as soon as she is on the street. "I hate to wear it," she says and stuffs it into her emergency bag.

"We're going to be late," Riko tells Sachi. Lunches and emergency bags bouncing, the two girls start to run.

At the corner, Riko makes Sachi stop. "Don't forget to wear your hood," she reminds her sister.

Sachi hurries to school and gathers in the yard with her classmates. They will not study in the classroom today. As members of the labor service corps, they have been assigned tasks outdoors

WORK

to help defend Japan against the American invasion.

The older children work in the factories. Others, like Riko, record phone messages at the army headquarters, located in an old castle. They have taken the place of the soldiers who are needed to fight the Americans.

Sachi and her classmates work outside in the streets tearing down houses. It is a sad sight for the owners, but they know it is necessary to lose their houses to support the war effort.

❦

Many of the Japanese buildings are wood and paper. In other cities, American planes have dropped bombs and started fires that have devastated large areas. As yet, this has not happened to Hiroshima, but since no one wants to take chances, the army and city officials have decided to make fire lanes. The empty spaces will help stop the fires from spreading. The lanes will also provide avenues for fire-fighting equipment as well as escape routes for people fleeing the flames.

Sachi and her classmates help the adults wreck houses. They sort through the remains, looking for useful parts they can save and reuse, such as roof tiles. It is hot, dusty work and the muggy air makes the dust stick to their sweaty faces. To make the work go faster, the children chant in time as they wield their shovels.

WORK

Sachi's best friend pulls on white gloves to protect her hands. Several children tie headbands around their foreheads to keep the sweat from their eyes.

Everyone is busy as the *Enola Gay* approaches.

**THE
ATTACK**

All over Japan, there are observers who look out for the American bombers. Nineteen miles east of Hiroshima, an observer spots the *Enola Gay* and its two companions. Hurriedly, he calls the army headquarters in Hiroshima.

Riko answers the phone and takes down the report. She is shocked to learn that there are more bombers coming.

Angrily, she thinks it is a sneaky trick to catch people outside the shelters.

She dials the radio station immediately and asks the announcers to warn everyone.

Riko thinks she is safe deep inside the ancient castle. But she prays for her mother at home and Sachi out in the street tearing down houses.

In the meantime, people go on calmly with their lives. They eat their breakfasts. They begin their work. Outside their homes, the very small children begin to play. A colonel rides his horse across a bridge.

❧

On the *Enola Gay*, Colonel Tibbets orders, "On glasses." His crew pull on goggles to protect their eyes. However,

Colonel Tibbets must see clearly to steer the bomber. He does not put on goggles. Neither does the bombardier.

Everyone is tense and excited. No one is sure if the bomb will go off. Yesterday on Tinian, Colonel Tibbets tested the gunlike device that sets off the bomb. It did not work then.

Now the bombardier looks through his bombsight and guides the *Enola Gay* the last few miles to its target.

Doors snap open on the belly of the plane.

The bombardier sees his landmark. It is a bridge shaped like a T. On the bridge, a Japanese colonel rides his horse.

The bombardier presses a button to release the bomb.

THE ATTACK

Down below, the children in the streets hear the hum of *Enola Gay*'s engines. They look up and see the *Enola Gay*. Its silver sides gleam in the sun. Fine white lines stripe the sky behind its engines. Sachi's friend calls excitedly to her and points up. "A B-29!"

"B-29! B-29!" a teacher shouts.

Sachi remembers her sister's warning. From her emergency bag, she pulls out her special hood and puts it on.

Another teacher blows a whistle. It is a signal for the children to go to the air-raid shelter.

❀

In the *Enola Gay*, the bombardier shouts, "Bomb away!"

The huge, heavy bomb drops from the airplane. Suddenly the *Enola Gay* is much lighter, and it jerks up into the air. Colonel Tibbets is skillful. He keeps control of the airplane and swings it to the right.

The bomb whistles as it plunges down, down through the air.

On the *Enola Gay,* a crewman flips a switch on a special radio. It sends a signal to a special gun inside the bomb.

This time the gun works. It shoots a cone-shaped bullet of uranium into a larger ball of uranium.

❦

Everything is made up of tiny particles called atoms. They are so small they are invisible to the eye. The atoms are also made up of even smaller parts. Energy holds these parts together like

18

glue. When the atom breaks up into its parts, the energy goes free and there is a big explosion.

Inside the bomb, one uranium atom collides with another. Those atoms both break up. Their parts smash into more atoms and split them in turn.

This is called a chain reaction. There are millions and millions of atoms inside the bomb. When they all break up, it is believed that the atom bomb will be equal to 20,000 tons of dynamite. In 1945, it is the most powerful weapon ever made.

☙

As the chain reaction builds, the bomb falls faster and faster. But it does not go off over the bridge. It explodes over a hospital instead.

HIROSHIMA

There is a blinding light like a sun.

There is a boom like a giant drum.

There is a terrible wind. Houses collapse like boxes. Windows break everywhere. Broken glass swirls like angry insects.

The wind strikes Sachi back like a hammer and picks her up. She feels as if she has fallen into boiling oil. It tears away her special hood and even her clothes. The wind sweeps her into the whirlwind of glass.

There is no time to scream. There is no one to hear.

There is only the darkness. . . .

And Sachi mercifully passes out.

THE
MUSHROOM
CLOUD

The *Enola Gay* circles. The same wind that carries Sachi through the air almost knocks the bomber from the sky. Colonel Tibbets manages to right his airplane. The two companion bombers begin to take pictures and record the explosion.

Up until then, no single bomb has

ever caused so much damage or so many deaths.

Out of 76,327 buildings, over 50,000 are destroyed.

Up to 125,000 people will die on that first day or will die soon.

The wind mixes their dust with the dirt and debris. Then it sends everything boiling upward in a tall purple-gray column. When the top of the dust cloud spreads out, it looks like a strange, giant mushroom.

The bottom of the mushroom cloud is a fiery red. All over the city fires spring up. They rise like flames from a bed of coals.

The bomb goes off 580 meters above the ground. The temperature reaches several million degrees Celsius immediately. It is so hot that the hospital below and everyone inside it disappears.

Two hundred yards away, people vanish. However, in that instant, their outlines are burnt into the cement like shadows.

The army headquarters and all the soldiers and Riko and her classmates are destroyed.

One mile away, the fierce heat starts fires.

Even two miles away, people are burned by the heat.

❦

On the *Enola Gay*, the tail gunner tries to count the fires. But he gives up because there are too many.

Everyone in the crew has flown on

bombers. They have helped drop tons of regular bombs. On each flight, they have seen death and destruction.

But no one has ever seen anything as powerful as this one bomb.

The copilot writes a note to himself: "What have we done?"

When the bomb's uranium breaks up, bits of atoms zip away. They go right through people's skin and hurt their bodies inside. This is called radiation. It will make thousands of people sick. Many will die later that day. More will fall ill and die in a year. Some will die in five years, or ten, or twenty. People are still dying today.

DESTRUCTION

Sachi wakes a few minutes later when she hears someone screaming. At first, there is so much smoke and dust she feels as if she is staring at a black wall. Then the smoke and dust rise like a curtain. She is stunned when she sees all the damage. One moment there was a city here. Now all the buildings are destroyed. The streets are filled with rubble and ruins. She does not know what could cause such wide destruction.

Shocked, Sachi stumbles through the wasteland until she stops upon a lawn. From the wrecked buildings, people call for help. Before she can help anyone, the buildings go up in flames.

It is so hot around her that the grass catches fire. She crouches down and waits and hopes. The sheet of fire retreats. Flames shoot out of the nearby houses. People continue to scream. Everywhere, there is a sea of fire.

Sachi follows some people as they run into a cemetery. She jumps over tombstones. The pine trees around them catch fire with a great crackling noise.

Ahead she sees a river. People jump into it to get away from the fire. In the panic, some people are crushed. Others drown. Sachi cannot swim. She jumps in anyway. Then she sees a wooden bucket drifting by. She grabs it and holds on desperately.

Soon the water is full of bodies.

The hot ash from all the fires soars high, high into the sky. When the fiery ash mixes with the cold air, it causes rain. It is a horrible kind of rain.

The rain falls in drops as big as marbles. The drops are black and greasy with dust. The drops sting like falling pebbles.

The rain leaves black, oily spots wherever it falls.

The rain is radioactive. It will make people sick, too. They will also die.

After about an hour, the rain puts out the fires. Somebody finds Sachi and brings her to the hospital.

HIROSHIMA

The people living just outside Hiro-shima think they are safe. They search through the deadly wasteland for family and friends. They do not know about radiation. Some of these searchers will also fall ill. Many of them will die.

One mother hunts all over the city for her children. Finally, she stops at a hospital.

The bodies of schoolchildren are piled up on a hallway bench. The mother looks through the bodies for her daughter. She hears a groan. Someone is alive. It is Sachi.

However, Sachi has terrible burns on her face. She cannot even smile. It is as if she has no face. One arm is bent permanently. Of all her classmates, only she has survived.

🪷

DESTRUCTION

Despite America's terrible new weapon, Japanese military leaders still refuse to give up.

Three days later, on August 9, 1945, the Americans drop another bomb, this time on the city of Nagasaki. Much of that city is also destroyed. Seventy thousand people die.

At last, on August 15, Japan surrenders. World War II is finally over.

THE HIROSHIMA MAIDENS

Sachi's father does not return home with the other surviving soldiers. He has died on an island in the Pacific. However, the war does not end for Hiroshima. Radiation kills many people that year.

Though Sachi and her mother survive, many of their friends and neighbors die, and radiation will kill even more people over the coming years. People are still dying today.

Sachi still carries her scars. For three years, she hides inside her house. All around her, she can hear the city being rebuilt and new people moving in.

Flowers bloom again. Some are as beautiful as ever. However, the radiation makes other flowers grow in strange, weird shapes.

When Sachi goes outside, she usually wears a doctor's mask to cover her scarred face. One time she does not and meets some children who have come to the city recently. The newcomers tease her because of the burns on her face and arm. They call her a monkey.

People are afraid of those who lived

through the bomb. They avoid the survivors. They think that the survivors may be weird in some way, like the odd flowers.

In 1949, a New York magazine editor, Norman Cousins, visits Hiroshima. He and others become interested in helping the victims of Hiroshima. Though thousands of people need surgery, they decide to start with a small group. The Americans and the Japanese work together. They choose twenty-five women. The American newspapers call the young women "the Hiroshima Maidens."

Many people are determined to help the Maidens. American surgeons will donate their time. American families will provide homes for the Maidens while they receive treatment.

The women leave Hiroshima on an American military transport plane.

Remembering the American plane that hurt so many people, they are frightened at first. When a soldier tries to serve a cold drink to Sachi, she shakes her head nervously. Another soldier offers her a wet towel to cool herself off. Again she refuses.

Finally, one soldier tries to speak Japanese to Sachi. He knows only a few basic words so he talks in simple sentences like a baby. That makes Sachi smile. She tries to chat with him, but it is hard.

Then Sachi remembers a book each of the women has been given. She takes it out to show him. It is a book of campfire songs. Though she cannot read English, she recognizes the musical notes.

She points to the first word. He pronounces it for her. She repeats it until he nods approvingly.

When they have gone through the first page, Sachi slowly tries to sing. The soldier quickly joins in. The other women take out their songbooks. Soon everyone is singing.

When the Maidens finally arrive in New York in May 1955, everything is strange and new to them. The food is very different. So are the customs. One woman wants to know where the cowboys are.

Sachi stays with an American family. She is afraid at first. However, she tries to act like a good Japanese daughter. Her American hosts begin to think of her as one of their own.

Every night she writes down new English words she learns because she wants to talk with her American friends. In turn, she teaches her new friends some of the games she played as a child. It helps occupy her during the recovery from the many operations on her face and arm.

On a television show, one of the crewmen from the *Enola Gay* sees two of the Maidens. He breaks into tears when he sees what happened to them.

Over 18 months, 138 free operations are performed on the 25 women. It is a long, painful process. And the surgery is not always successful. One Maiden even dies, but the other women go on bravely with the operations.

For the doctors, it is a labor of good-will. For the women, it is a matter of trust and hope.

In the end, Sachi has made many friends in the United States. They are sorry to see her go.

Like other children, she has survived the war and its painful memories. Now her suffering has made her understand the suffering of others. She wants to help those victims still at home.

At a farewell dinner she is asked to speak. First, she lifts her left arm proudly into the air. She tells the audience in a quiet voice that for years she was unable to use that arm. Now she can hold it up straight. For years she hid in her house. Now she is able to smile at the world once again. She is ready to start a new life.

Sachi and the other Maidens return to Japan. With them, they take the ashes of the woman who died. They refer to themselves as the Azalea Club because azaleas bloom in May. And May is the month that they arrived in the United States.

However, in Japan not everyone approves of the project. They think all the money spent on the Maidens should have been spent on Hiroshima instead.

Because of the controversy, no more survivors leave for the United States. Instead, the Japanese build special hospitals for them. And in 1957, their homeland begins to pass laws to help the victims.

PEACE?

After Hiroshima, war takes on a new, terrible meaning. Everyone is afraid of the powerful atomic weapon. And four years after Hiroshima, the Soviet Union announces that it has made its own atom bomb. The United States immediately decides to make a bigger, more powerful bomb. People all over the world begin to worry that the United

States will go to war with the Soviet Union.

In schools all across the United States, children practice what to do during an attack. They hide under their desks in case the Soviets drop their atom bombs. And in their backyards, families dig big holes. In the holes, they build concrete rooms where they can live through an atomic attack.

Great Britain develops its own atom bomb. At first, the countries test their atom bombs in the open, and the wind spreads the radiation. On March 1, 1954, Japanese fishermen become sick after an American test. One of the fishermen dies. Great Britain, the Soviet Union, and the United States promise not to test any more bombs in the air. They agree to test them underground. It takes nine years to reach an agreement. In the meantime, France makes its own atom bomb, but does not sign the treaty. Other countries also refuse to sign the treaty. Some of them, like China, want to create their own atom bomb.

All these bombs cost a lot of money. The United States alone has paid 750 billion dollars for around 60,000 weapons and for bombers and missiles to take them to their targets.

Each year there are newer and improved weapons such as cruise missiles that can fly low to the ground. They are hard to detect. Inside the cruise missiles are computers that guide them to their targets.

On December 8, 1987, the United States and the Soviet Union agree to destroy all of their medium-range missiles. These missiles could travel up to

PEACE?

3400 miles. Inspectors from each country would check to make sure the missiles had been destroyed. It takes six years to dismantle all of them.

Since then, the Soviet Union has broken up into several republics. The larger republics — such as Russia, the Ukraine, and Kazakhstan — have stockpiles of atomic weapons. The United States and the republics have agreed to destroy some of their weapons.

Already, many countries are suspected of being capable of making atom bombs. Still others already have or are getting ready to produce their own. Among these are India, Iraq, Israel, North Korea, and Pakistan.

Some of these weapons are now thousands of times as powerful as the Hiroshima bomb.

There are still enough bombs to destroy the world many times over.

And if only half the atomic weapons were set off, many scientists believe they would create enough smoke and dust to hide the sun. The day would never get brighter than twilight. It would create a special kind of winter all over the world. The cold would kill plants everywhere. So, even in places where the bomb did not drop, people and animals would starve to death.

Scientists say that if the bombs drop again, no one will win because no one will survive.

All life on Earth will end.

While fear has made some governments want atom bombs, fear has also made some people think. They want peace without nuclear weapons.

In 1985, 40 years after the bomb

PEACE?

dropped, people all around the world marched for peace. In the capital, Washington, D.C., many thousands of people carried banners with peace messages and symbols. Stitched together, the banners formed a peace ribbon 15 miles long.

THE
PARK

Today there is a park in Hiroshima where the bomb dropped. Near the park is a museum. It opened in 1955 and houses some 6000 items left after the explosion.

Each year 1,200,000 people visit the museum. They look at the photos and exhibits. And they examine the twisted roof tiles and melted bottles. They are strange, disturbing relics of that terrible moment.

Japan has built a new wing to the museum. The new exhibit includes Japan's role in World War II and shows how the city of Hiroshima participated in the military effort. For the first time, the bombing is placed in an historical context.

Also in the park is the Atomic Bomb Dome. It shelters a coffin made of stone. Inside the coffin is a list of all those who have died because the bomb dropped on Hiroshima. Radiation has taken thousands more lives besides those who died on the first day of the explosion.

Every year on August 6, more names are added to the list. Forty years after the bomb dropped, there were 125,000 names on the list. Four thousand to five thousand names have been added each year after that.

Carved on the monument are the words:

"Rest in peace
for the mistake shall not be repeated."

In 1955, a little girl called Sadako got sick from radiation. She had heard a legend that if she folded one thousand paper cranes, she would get her wish. Wanting to wish for life, she began to fold paper into cranes. But her wish did not come true. Sadako died ten years after the bomb had dropped.

THE PARK

Sadako's schoolmates were so shocked at her death that they helped raise money to build a monument to her memory. At the very top stands a life-size statue of Sadako. She holds a gold-colored crane over her head. Below, on either side, are statues of a boy and girl flying through the air. The monument is dedicated to all the children of Hiroshima who died because of the bomb.

About the time that Sadako died, some high school girls in Hiroshima organized the Paper Crane Club. They started folding paper into cranes just as Sadako did. It was their way of remembering her and all the other young victims of Hiroshima.

Each year, children from around the world send as many as 400 million paper cranes to Hiroshima. String is threaded through the cranes and they are hung beneath Sadako's statue in thick layers.

And every year on August 6, people come to the park for a special ceremony. As night falls, they go to the river that was once full of bodies. In their hands, they carry candles inside of paper boxes.

Sachi is there, too. On the softly colored sides of the candle box, she has written the names of her father and sister. She lights the candle and sets the box on the water. Quickly it moves away from her.

The currents swirl the candle boxes together like flocks of glowing pastel

THE PARK

birds. Bobbing up and down on the river, the candle boxes float out toward the dark sea and into the night itself. And, as the tiny lights drift into the blackness, the people pray that others around the world will remember Hiroshima and work for world peace.

The atom bomb is too terrible a weapon.

It must not drop again.

AFTERWORD

Sachi is a composite of several children who were in Hiroshima when the bomb dropped and who later came to the United States. We should all draw lessons from their suffering and their courage.

In telling their story, I have never had so much trouble resolving statistical conflicts. For instance, at the time the atom bomb was dropped on Hiroshima, it was reported to be a twenty kiloton bomb. Today, most authorities agree that it was actually a thirteen kiloton bomb.

Because of civilian evacuations and troop movements, there are no definite figures for the population in Hiroshima at the time of the atomic bombing. The scope and scale of the destruction has also made it impossible to be sure how many people actually died that day.

The death figures are based on findings published in *Hiroshima and Nagasaki: The Physical, Medical and Social Effects of the Atomic Bombings*. Written by the Committee for the Compilation of Materials on Damage Caused by the Atomic Bombs in Hiroshima and Nagasaki, this is considered to be the most authoritative source on the bombings.

AFTERWORD

The official damage statistics for Hiroshima and Nagasaki also vary, and the truth will probably never be known. I have cited damage figures based on the official surveys of both cities as quoted in *Hiroshima and Nagasaki.*

L.Y.

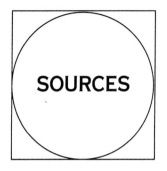

SOURCES

Barker, Rodney. *Hiroshima Maidens*. New York: Viking, 1985.

Committee for the Compilation of Materials on Damage Caused by the Atomic Bombs in Hiroshima and Nagasaki. *Hiroshima and Nagasaki: The Physical, Medical and Social Effects of the Atomic Bombings*. Trans. Eisei Ishikawa and David L. Swain. New York: Basic Books, 1981.

SOURCES

Del Tredici, Robert. *At Work in the Fields of the Bomb*. New York: Harper & Row, 1987.

Gigon, Fernand. *The Bomb*. Trans. Constantine Fitz Gibbon. New York: Pyramid Books, 1960.

Hersey, John. *Hiroshima*. New York: Alfred A. Knopf, 1985.

Hiroshima Jogakuin High School. English Department. trans. *Summer Cloud*. Tokyo: San-yu-sha, n.d.

Huie, William Bradford. *The Hiroshima Pilot*. New York: G.P. Putnam & Sons, 1964.

Kome, Penney and Patrick Crean, eds. *Peace, A Dream Unfolding*. San Francisco: Sierra Club, 1986.

Lifton, Betty Jean and Eikoh Hosoe. *Return to Hiroshima*. New York: Kodansha, 1984.

Lifton, Robert Jay. *Death in Life*. New York: Random House, 1967.

SOURCES

Lloyd, Alwyn. *B-29 Superfortress, Production Versions*. Blue Ridge, PA: TAB Books, 1983.

―――. B-29 Superfortress, Part 2, *Derivatives*. Blue Ridge, PA: TAB Books, 1987.

MacPherson, Malcolm C. *Time Bomb*. New York: E.P. Dutton, 1986.

Oe, Kenzaburo. *Hiroshima Notes*. Trans. Toshi Yonezawa; Ed. David L. Swain. Tokyo: YMCA Press, 1981.

Osada, Arata. *Children of Hiroshima*. London: Taylor and Francis; Tokyo: Publishing Committee for "Children of Hiroshima," 1980.

Pimlott, John. *B-29 Superfortress*. Secaucus, NJ: Chartwell Books, 1980.

Rhodes, Richard. *The Making of the Atomic Bomb*. New York: Simon & Schuster, 1986.

Thomas, Gordon and Morgan Witts. *Enola Gay*. New York: Pyramid Books, 1977.

SOURCES

Time-Life Books. *The Aftermath: Asia.* New York: Time-Life Books, 1983.

———. *Japan at War.* New York: Time-Life Books, 1980.

Wheeler, Peter. *Bombers Over Japan.* New York: Time-Life Books, 1982.

Wyden, Peter. *Day One.* New York: Simon & Schuster, 1984.

🏵

In addition, specialists at the National Air and Space Museum of the Smithsonian Institution and the National Atomic Museum were consulted, as well as articles in *The New York Times, San Francisco Chronicle, San Francisco Examiner,* and items in Facts on File World News Digest.